HONDURAS

DISCOVERING CENTRAL AMERICA
History, Politics, and Culture

HONDURAS

Charles J. Shields

Mason Crest
Philadelphia

Mason Crest
450 Parkway Drive, Suite D
Broomall, PA 19008
www.masoncrest.com

CPSIA Compliance Information: Batch #DCA2015.
For further information, contact Mason Crest at 1-866-MCP-Book.

First printing
1 3 5 7 9 8 6 4 2

Library of Congress Cataloging-in-Publication Data
on file at the Library of Congress

ISBN: 978-1-4222-3290-3 (hc)
ISBN: 978-1-4222-8656-2 (ebook)

Discovering Central America: History, Politics, and Culture series ISBN: 978-1-4222-3284-2

DISCOVERING CENTRAL AMERICA: History, Politics, and Culture

Belize
Central America: Facts and Figures
Costa Rica
El Salvador

Guatemala
Honduras
Nicaragua
Panama

Table of Contents

KEY ICONS TO LOOK FOR:

Words to Understand: These words with their easy-to-understand definitions will increase the reader's understanding of the text, while building vocabulary skills.

Sidebars: This boxed material within the main text allows readers to build knowledge, gain insights, explore possibilities, and broaden their perspectives by weaving together additional information to provide realistic and holistic perspectives.

Research Projects: Readers are pointed toward areas of further inquiry connected to each chapter. Suggestions are provided for projects that encourage deeper research and analysis.

Text-Dependent Questions: These questions send the reader back to the text for more careful attention to the evidence presented there.

Series Glossary of Key Terms: This back-of-the book glossary contains terminology used throughout this series. Words found here increase the reader's ability to read and comprehend higher-level books and articles in this field.

Discovering Central America

James D. Henderson

CENTRAL AMERICA is a beautiful part of the world, filled with generous and friendly people. It is also a region steeped in history, one of the first areas of the New World explored by Christopher Columbus. Central America is both close to the United States and strategically important to it. For nearly a century ships of the U.S. and the world have made good use of the Panama Canal. And for longer than that breakfast tables have been graced by the bananas and other tropical fruits that Central America produces in abundance.

Central America is closer to North America and other peoples of the world with each passing day. Globalized trade brings the region's products to world markets as never before. And there is promise that trade agreements will soon unite all nations of the Americas in a great common market. Meanwhile improved road and air links make it easy for visitors to reach Middle America. Central America's tropical flora and fauna are ever more accessible to foreign visitors having an interest in eco-tourism. Other visitors are drawn to the region's dazzling Pacific Ocean beaches, jewel-like scenery, and bustling towns and cities. And everywhere Central America's wonderful and varied peoples are outgoing and welcoming to foreign visitors.

These eight books are intended to provide complete, up-to-date information on the five countries historians call Central America (Guatemala, El Salvador, Honduras, Nicaragua, Costa Rica), as well as on Panama (technically part of South America) and Belize (technically part of North America). Each volume contains chapters on the land, history, economy, people, and cultures of the countries treated. And each country study is written in an engaging style, employing a vocabulary appropriate to young students.

Hondurans wait for a bus outside a village market.

All volumes contain colorful illustrations, maps, and up-to-date boxed information of a statistical character, and each is accompanied by a chronology, a glossary, a bibliography, selected Internet resources, and an index. Students and teachers alike will welcome the many suggestions for individual and class projects and reports contained in each country study, and they will want to prepare the tasty traditional dishes described in each volume's recipe section.

This eight-book series is a timely and useful addition to the literature on Central America. It is designed not just to inform, but also to engage school-aged readers with this important and fascinating part of the Americas.

Let me introduce this series as author Charles J. Shields begins each volume: *¡Hola!* You are discovering Central America!

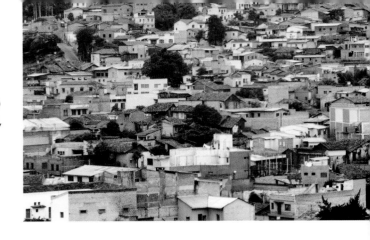

(Opposite) Thatched huts stand under palm trees on a beach in a Miskito village. The Miskito are a tribe of people who are native to Honduras. (Right) Densely packed houses in Tegucigalpa, the capital of Honduras. The city's population grew very quickly during the second half of the 20th century.

1 Honduras—The Knee of Central America

¡HOLA! ARE YOU DISCOVERING Honduras? It is the second-largest country in Central America after Nicaragua and is rich in natural beauty, history, culture, and hospitality. The climate ranges from the cool, mountainous interior to the warm Caribbean coastline. The attractions of this land are spectacular, including the ancient Mayan ruins of Copán; the picturesque Bay Islands in the Caribbean; the charming Caribbean coastal towns of La Ceiba, Tela, and Trujillo; the rugged beauty of the Pacific coastline; and the lush *cloud forests*, such as La Tigra. Tegucigalpa (population 1.25 million), the capital of Honduras, retains the look of *colonial* times in some neighborhoods, yet offers all the conveniences of a small city.

Honduras is the knee of Central America—bordered to the south by Nicaragua and El Salvador and on the west by Guatemala. It has a 399 mile long (644 kilometer) Caribbean coastline and a tiny 77 mile (124 km) Pacific coastline. The Caribbean Bay Islands and further northeast, the distant Swan Islands, are both part of Honduran territory.

Three-quarters of Honduras is composed of rugged hills and mountains, ranging from 984 to 9,348 feet (300 to 2,850 meters) in height. Lowlands are found only along the coasts and in major river valleys. Deforestation is occurring at a rate of 1,170 square miles (3,000 sq. km.) a year because of a demand for beef. Farmers cut down forests to create grassland for grazing. If this continues, Honduras will become a muddy,

Words to Understand in this Chapter

cloud forest—a wet, tropical forest that has clouds surrounding it even in the dry season.

colonial—having to do with one country using the resources of another.

erosion—the act of wearing away, usually dirt or rocks.

lagoon—a coastal body of shallow water formed where low-lying rock, sand, or coral presents a partial barrier to the open sea.

lumbering—to cut down the trees in a region and convert them into saleable lumber.

mangrove—tropical tree that has an extensive root system and is important to land-building.

pesticide—a chemical substance used to kill pests, especially insects.

savanna—a flat grassland, sometimes with scattered trees, in a tropical or subtropical region.

sorghum—a cereal plant that is resistant to drought, widely cultivated in tropical and warm areas as a grain crop and for animal feed.

topographical—how land is shown on maps.

treeless landscape within the next 20 years. However, there are still largely untouched areas, especially in the Mosquitia region. Animals that roam the hidden regions include jaguars, armadillos, wild pigs, monkeys and alligators. Abundant bird life, such as toucans, herons and kingfishers, still can be seen, too.

The Land: Three Different Regions

Honduras has three different *topographical* regions—a large interior highland area and two narrow coastal lowlands. The interior highlands, which make up nearly 80 percent of the country's terrain, is mountainous. The mountain ranges generally run from west to east, but some valleys wander north and south, such as the large Comayagua Valley of central Honduras. The larger Caribbean lowlands in the north and the Pacific lowlands bordering the Golfo de Fonseca are mainly broad, wet plains.

Interior Highlands

The interior highlands are the chief feature of Honduran topography and are home to most of the population. However, because the rugged terrain has made both travel and farming difficult, this area has not been highly developed. The generally fertile soils, containing lava and volcanic ash, produce coffee, tobacco, wheat, corn, *sorghum*, beans, fruits, and vegetables. Farmers also raise cattle, poultry, and pigs.

In the western area of the interior highlands, Honduras's mountains blend into the mountain ranges of Guatemala. The western mountains have the highest peaks, with Pico Congolón at an elevation of 8,200 feet (2,500 m) and the Cerro de Las Minas at 9,349 feet (2,850 m). Pine forests cover the slopes of these mountains. In the east, the mountains merge with those in Nicaragua. Although generally not as high as the mountains near the Guatemalan border, the eastern ranges thrust up some tall peaks, such as the Montaña de la Flor, Monte El Boquerón, and Pico Bonito—all over 8,000 feet (2,439 m).

Scattered throughout the interior highlands are numerous flat-floored valleys. The floors of the large valleys provide grassland to support livestock and, in some cases, commercial agriculture. On the slopes of the valleys, farmers are able to raise only enough food to feed their families, relying on simple tools and their own hard labor. Villages and towns, including the capital, Tegucigalpa, are tucked into the larger valleys.

Vegetation in the interior highlands varies from pine forests on the western, southern, and central mountains to evergreen forests on the eastern ranges. Clinging to the highest peaks are the last patches of dense rain forest that once covered much of the highlands.

Caribbean Lowlands

The Caribbean lowlands, which most Hondurans call "the north coast," is a narrow coastal plain only a few miles wide occupying about one-fifth of the total land area of the country. Hot and humid, the Caribbean lowlands are densely forested in the interior—*lumbering* is an important economic activity. To the east and west of this section, the lowlands widen and jut into broad river valleys. The broadest river valley, along the Río Ulúa near the Guatemalan border, is Honduras's most developed sector. Two economically

Quick Facts: The Geography of Honduras

Location: Middle America, bordering the Caribbean Sea between Guatemala and Nicaragua and bordering the North Pacific Ocean between El Salvador and Nicaragua.

Geographic coordinates: 15'00" N, 86'30"W

Area: (slightly larger than Tennessee)
 total: 112,090 sq. km
 land: 111,890 sq. km
 water: 200 sq. km

Borders: Guatemala (256 km), El Salvador (342 km), Nicaragua (922 km).

Terrain: mostly mountains in interior, narrow coastal plains.

Elevation extremes:
 lowest point: Caribbean Sea 0 m
 highest point: Cerro Las Minas 2,870 m

Natural resources: timber, gold, silver, copper, lead, zinc, iron ore, antimony, coal, fish, hydropower.

Source: CIA World Factbook 2015

important places are located here—Puerto Cortés, the country's largest port, and San Pedro Sula, Honduras's industrial and agricultural center.

To the far east, near the Nicaraguan border, the Caribbean lowlands fan out into a humid, bug-infested area known as the Mosquitia, or the Mosquito Coast. Consisting of inland *savanna* with swamps and *mangrove*, the Mosquitia is Honduras's least developed area. During times of heavy rainfall, the few people who live here get around by shallow-draft boats. Farming and fishing are the main occupations of the scattered population.

Pacific Lowlands

The Pacific lowlands, centered on the Gulf of Fonseca, are only a small part of Honduras and contain an equally small part of the population. The land is flat, changing to swamps near the shores of the gulf. But the soil there is rich because it washes down from the mountain slopes. Farms in the Pacific lowlands produce sesame seed, cotton, and some corn and sorghum. Cattle graze in the lowland pastures, and coffee is grown on the nearby uplands. Fishing in the gulf is good for two reasons: First, the water is shallow and attracts fish and mollusks. Second, mangroves along the shore provide safe breeding grounds for shrimp and shellfish that live among the trees' roots.

Several islands in the gulf belong to Honduras. The two largest—Zacate Grande and El Tigre—are eroded volcanoes, part of the chain of volcanoes that extends along the Pacific coast of Central America. Both islands have volcanic cones that rise more than 2,296 feet (700 m). Ship captains use them as markers showing the way to Honduras's Pacific ports.

A Water-Rich Country

Honduras is a water-rich country. Numerous rivers, which have carved broad, fertile valleys, drain the interior highlands and empty to the north into the Caribbean. The downstream portions of these rivers near the Caribbean will float shallow-draft boats, but upstream from the first rapids at the foot of the mountains, only dugout canoes can be used for local travel and commerce. The major rivers in Honduras are the Ulúa, Aguán, Negro, Platano, Patuca, and, on the Nicaragua border, the Rio Coco, the largest in Central America. Economically, the most important river is the Ulúa, which flows 672 miles (400 km) through the Valle de Sula.

Rivers also define about half of Honduras's international borders. The Río Goascorán, flowing to the Golfo de Fonseca, and the Río Lempa create the border between El Salvador and Honduras. The Río Coco marks about half of the border between Nicaragua and Honduras.

Although rivers are plentiful in Honduras, large bodies of water are rare. Lago de Yojoa, located in the west-central part of the country, is the only natural lake in country. It is 37 miles (22 km) long and 23 miles across (14 km) at its widest point. Several large, muddy *lagoons* open onto the Caribbean in northeast Honduras, allowing limited transportation by boat to points along the coast.

Inside the Hurricane Belt

All of Honduras lies within the tropics, but the mountains create variety in the climate. Land below 3,280 feet (1,000 m) is commonly known as *tierra caliente* (hot land); between 3,280 and 6,560 feet (1,000 and 2,000 m) is the *tierra templada* (temperate land); and above 6,560 feet (2,000 m) is the *tierra*

A panoramic view of the mountains and rainforests of northeastern Honduras.

fría (cold land).

Each of these three main regions in Honduras has a slightly different climate. The Caribbean lowlands have a tropical, wet climate with high temperatures and humidity. Rain falls fairly regularly throughout the year here. The Pacific lowlands have a tropical, wet climate with high temperatures, too, but also a dry season from November through April. Also at that time of year, the interior highlands have a dry season, but temperatures drop as the land rises to the mountains. Overall, the interior is much cooler than the humid coast. Temperatures in the capital Tegucigalpa, for example, range between 77° and 86° F (25 and 30° C).

Honduras lies within the hurricane belt, and the Caribbean coast is especially susceptible to hurricanes or tropical storms that travel inland from the Caribbean. In 1982, Tropical Storm Alleta flooded thousands of people and caused extensive damage to crops. Hurricane Fifi killed more than 8,000 people and destroyed nearly the entire banana crop in 1974. In 1998, Honduras was hit extremely hard by Hurricane Mitch, causing loss of life in the thousands.

Plants and Animals

In eastern Honduras, the coastal and lagoon swamps have mangrove and palm forests. West of these are low, rainy, sandy plains with pine savanna, stretching inland for 40 miles (65 km) or more. Further west of the pine savanna, in low valleys and on lower mountains which are rainy all year, are broad belts of dense evergreen forests. Many species of large trees live here—mahogany, Spanish cedar, balsa, rosewood, ceiba, sapodilla, and castilloa rubber. The high, rainy mountain slopes of the Honduras highlands support excellent forests of oak and pine.

Insects, birds, and reptiles are the most often-seen creatures in Honduras. Waterfowl in large numbers inhabit the coastal areas. Crocodiles, snakes, turtles, and lizards, including giant iguana and others, are found in the tropical forest areas. Other animals include deer, peccaries, tapir, pumas, jaguars, and ocelots. Fish and mollusks are abundant in lagoons and coastal waters.

Honduras faces some serious environmental problems, however. Deforestation has led to extensive soil *erosion*. Also, *pesticides* used by banana growers have caused environmental damage in coastal regions. To safeguard native plants and animals, the Honduras government established national parks, protected forests, and biological reserves in the late 1980s and 1990s. Mount Azul de Copán National Park (established in 1987), for example, is an area of rain forest that surrounds the famous Mayan ruins of Copán. La Tigra National Park, established in 1980, covers 92 square miles (238 sq. km) of cloud forest near Tegucigalpa.

TEXT-DEPENDENT QUESTIONS

1. What are the three topographical regions of Honduras?
2. What is the highest mountain in Honduras?
3. What large lake is located in the west-central part of the country?

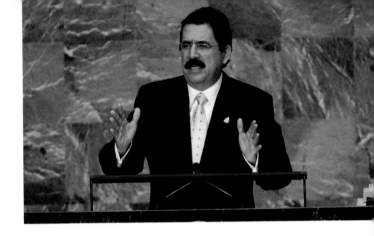

(Opposite) Tourists walk through the ancient Mayan city of Copán. The Maya lived in Honduras as early as 3,000 years ago. (Right) In 2009, the Honduran military removed President José Manuel Zelaya from office. The coup was widely condemned by the international community.

2 Honduras Becomes the "Banana Republic"

THE HISTORY OF Honduras has been largely shaped by the land itself. Because the region is rugged, with few natural resources, Honduras has been underpopulated since ancient times. The great Indian civilizations of the time flourished primarily to the north. Later, European expeditions reported unfavorably about the land and its resources. A strong and wealthy ruling class of colonial landowners never took hold and prospered. As a result, Honduran society today is less rigid and more democratic than most Central American countries.

However, Honduras's neighbors have taken advantage of the country's weaknesses to interfere in its affairs. Nations outside the region have tried to control Honduras to suit their interests. Honduras's formerly foreign-controlled economy and its United Fruit plantations, upset by periods of political unrest, gave rise to the unflattering term, "banana republic."

From the Mayans to the Colonial Period

Before the arrival of the Europeans, one of the most remarkable Indian groups in Honduras was the Maya, whose civilization spread south from the Yucatán and Guatemala. There is evidence of Maya settlement since at least 1000 BCE at Copán in western Honduras. For three-and-a-half centuries, Copán was one of the principal centers of Mayan culture and trade. Like other Maya city-states, however, it was mysteriously abandoned around 900 CE. The priests and rulers who built the temples, inscribed the *glyphs*, and developed the astronomy and mathematics suddenly vanished. The reason for this continues to puzzle archaeologists. Theories of civil war, disease, drought, overpopulation, and crop failure have all been suggested. Whatever the cause, the fall of the Mayan civilization seems to have affected only the city dwellers; the peasants remained in the area. Their languages and culture form links to the Mayan past.

Words to Understand in this Chapter

buccaneer—a pirate who preyed on Spanish colonies and shipping in the Caribbean region during the 17th century.

glyphs—pictures carved in stone that tell stories.

isthmus—narrow stretch of land with water on two sides.

In 1502, Columbus set foot on the American mainland for the first time at Trujillo in northern Honduras. He named the country after the deep water off the Caribbean coast—"Honduras" means "depths" in Italian, Columbus's native language.

Little exploration or settlement by Europeans took place for the two decades following Columbus' arrival. Then, Spanish conquistadors and a few settlers began arriving in the 1520s. Indians resisted Spanish colonialism, and, by some accounts, almost managed to drive the colonizers from the mainland. The chief of the Lenca tribe, Lempira, led 30,000 Indians against the Spanish, but he was treacherously murdered at peace talks in 1538. The Spanish crushed all Indian resistance within a year after that. The Indian population in the area dropped rapidly, almost wiped out by new diseases, mistreatment, and exportation to other colonies of large numbers of persons as slaves. By 1539, only about 15,000 native people remained under Spanish control. Two years later, this figure had declined to 8,000.

Adventurers discovered gold and silver near Tegucigalpa in 1570, attracting British and Dutch pirates to the Trujillo area. Around 1600, one Spanish military leader estimated that Roatan was home to 5,000 *buccaneers*.

By the 17th century, Honduras had become a poor and neglected backwater of Spain's colonial empire, having a scattered population of *mestizos*—persons of mixed European and native ancestry—native people, blacks, and a handful of Spanish administrators and landowners. Raising cattle was the only important economic activity, and much of the region remained outside Spanish control. Dutch pirates looted and burned Trujillo in 1643, and the Spanish did not resettle it until 1787.

In the early 19th century, Spanish power went into rapid decline. As Napoleon's armies marched across Europe, Spain was too deeply involved in war to pay much attention to Central America. As a result, the people of Spanish colonies used the opportunity to break away and become independent nations.

Independence and Strife

Spain granted independence to Honduras in 1821. Honduras briefly became part of independent Mexico, but then joined the Central American Federation in the early 1830s. But Spanish rule had fostered rivalry and suspicions among the five provinces of the federation. Constant fighting tore it apart, and in 1838, Honduras declared independence as a separate nation.

The years that followed were neither peaceful nor prosperous in Honduras. The country's weakness attracted the ambitions of individuals and nations both within and outside of Central America. The most infamous was the invasion by an American, William Walker, in 1860, whose attempt to take over Central America ended with defeat in Trujillo by an army of Hondurans, Nicaraguans, and Costa Ricans.

Even geography contributed to Honduras's misfortunes. Honduras is the only Central American republic to share land borders with three other nations: Guatemala, El Salvador, and Nicaragua. During the century and a half following Honduras's independence, civil wars throughout the *isthmus* spilled over borders. Honduran dictators tried to ally themselves with powerful neighbors, but takeovers and attempted takeovers of the government occurred frequently. The combined impact of civil strife and foreign interference kept Honduras in a state of economic and social backwardness for the next several decades.

Fruit Companies

The end of the 19th century and the first decades of the 20th century were a time of political and economic change in Honduras. The peaceful election of a president in 1899 was the first time that a legal transfer of power had taken place in decades. And in 1899, the first boatload of bananas from Honduras arrived in the United States. The

American companies such as United Fruit had a strong influence on the development of Honduras.

fruit found a ready market here, and the trade grew rapidly. Three U.S. companies—Standard Fruit, Cuyamel Fruit, and United Fruit—eventually owned 75 percent of all Honduran banana groves. Bananas accounted for 66 percent of all Honduran exports in 1913, making the companies powerful players in the Honduran economy.

These companies became very powerful in politics as well. Until the early 20th century, the United States had played only a limited role in Honduran political clashes. But with its investments in Honduras growing, the U.S. government monitored Honduras's political scene closely. From 1920 through 1923, there were 17 uprisings or attempted coups in Honduras. The U.S. Navy frequently sent warships to waters near Honduras to guard American business interests. This pressure had the desired result, and more stable governments came to power from 1925 to 1931.

Political stability did not result in long-term democracy. From 1932 to 1954, two dictators ruled Honduras in turn: Tiburcio Carías Andino and Juan Manuel Gálvez. These men used harsh measures to guarantee political calm. Then, a coup ousted the elected president in 1956 and marked a turning point in Honduran history. The Honduran military had taken a hand in the overthrow and would act as an "extra government" for decades, supervising the country's politics. Over the years, however, growing economic problems made the military regime increasingly unpopular. Except for a brief period in 1969, when the country united behind the military to fight the six-day Soccer War with El Salvador, pressure slowly mounted for a return to civilian, or non-military, government.

Honduran general Tiburcio Carías Andino dominated the nation's politics from the 1920s through the 1940s.

Conflicts with Neighboring Nations

In 1969, El Salvador accused the Honduran government of mistreating El Salvadoran emigrants living in Honduras. During a World Cup-qualifying soccer match between Honduras and El Salvador, El Salvadoran troops invaded Honduran territory and bombed Honduran airports. The Soccer War, which lasted only 100 hours, soured relations between the two neighbors for the next 10 years.

The two combatants formally signed a peace treaty on October 30,

A group of Contra rebels practice with a rocket launcher at their base camp near the Honduran border. During the 1980s the Contras waged a guerrilla war against the ruling Sandinista government of Nicaragua from bases in Honduras and Costa Rica.

1980, which put the dispute before the International Court of Justice. In September 1992, the court issued a 400-page ruling, awarding much of the land in question to Honduras.

During the 1980s, turmoil in Nicaragua, El Salvador, and Guatemala troubled Honduras. Following an overthrow of Nicaragua's dictator, National Guard troops still loyal to him, known as Contras, fled into Honduras. The United States government, trying to stop Communist movements in Central America, poured aid and military assistance into Honduras in an effort keep it stable. In addition, the United States military provided training to the Contras and El Salvadoran refugees living in Honduran camps. When the extent of United States involvement in Central American affairs was revealed—an estimated 12,000 Contras were operating from Honduras with American aid—anti-American demonstrations drew crowds of 60,000 in Tegucigalpa. The Honduran government finally reassessed its role as a U.S. military base, refused to sign a new military agreement with the United States, and ordered the Contras out of Honduras. With the election of a new president of Nicaragua in 1990, the war ended, and the Contras left Honduras.

Another Coup

In 2005 Manuel Zelaya was elected president of Honduras in a very close race. He took office in early 2006. During Zelaya's term in office, Honduras established closer ties with several socialist states, including Venezuela and Cuba.

In 2009, as his term neared an end, Zelaya proposed making changes to the Honduran constitution. His political opponents charged that he was looking to eliminate the limit on presidential terms, so that he could serve another term in office. The Supreme Court ruled that what Zelaya was doing was illegal, but the president pressed ahead anyway. On June 28, 2009, the military removed Zelaya from office and deported him to Costa Rica, a neutral country. The head of the Honduran Congress, Roberto Micheletti, became the interim president.

The international community strongly condemned the military's action as a coup d'état. Many countries broke off diplomatic ties with Honduras. Ultimately, democratic elections were held as scheduled in November 2009, with Porfirio "Pepe" Lobo Sosa being elected president. The new president investigated the constitutional crisis. He also arranged for Zelaya to return from the Dominican Republic, where he had been living in exile. With the resumption of democracy, the United States and other nations re-established ties and resumed their aid programs.

In 2014, Juan Orlando Hernández of the National Party was elected president of Honduras. He defeated Xiomara Castro, Zelaya's wife, who claimed that the result had been fraudulent.

Honduras remains a poor country. The average annual income of Hondurans is among the lowest in the Western Hemisphere. According to the United Nations Office on Drugs and Crime,

Juan Orlando Hernández speaks to the media from the presidential palace in Tegucigalpa.

Honduras has the highest murder rate in the world. Organized gangs have become involved in smuggling drugs into the United States and other countries. Given the grim social problems Honduras faces, it is not surprising that the country has seen civil unrest.

TEXT-DEPENDENT QUESTIONS

1. In what year were bananas from Honduras first shipped to the United States?
2. What military leader dominated Honduran politics from the 1920s through the 1940s?
3. What reason did Honduran military leaders give for removing President Zelaya from office in 2009?

(Opposite) A Honduran man carries bananas, one of the country's main export crops. About two-thirds of Hondurans are involved in banana or coffee farming. (Right) Carrying a basket of bread on her head, a woman walks past a hill that collapsed under rocks and mud in the La Colonia Soto neighborhood of Tegucigalpa.

3 A Fragile Economy

HONDURAS IS ONE OF the poorest countries in the Western Hemisphere. Since colonial times, the Honduran economy has relied on basic exports: minerals before 1900 and bananas and coffee throughout the 20th and 21st centuries. About two-thirds of Honduran workers are employed in agriculture. Changes in world prices for bananas and coffee affect jobs and people's livelihoods directly, and output from manufacturing remains low. Many basic problems face the economy, including rapid population growth, high unemployment, lack of farmable land, and too much dependence on coffee and bananas as exports. Honduras receives a large amount of foreign aid and technical assistance from the United States.

29

Few Resources

Since achieving independence in 1821, the economy of Honduras has largely depended on a handful of natural resources and on agriculture. Despite those hopes, usable land has always been severely limited due to the rugged *terrain*.

The economy is geographically divided between the interior highlands, where family farming, livestock raising, and mining have long been the main livelihoods, and the Pacific and Caribbean lowlands, where banana *plantations* employ the most workers. Food crops raised throughout Honduras include corn, beans, rice, and sugarcane, but bananas and coffee are the most important exports. Beef and seafood are exported, too. In recent years, shrimp and lobster farming have provided another important Honduran export.

During much of the 19th century, the Honduran economy did poorly. Cattle raising and family agriculture produced no major exports. In the latter part of the century, economic activity quickened with the develop-

Words to Understand in this Chapter

investors—person who puts money into a business.
maquiladoras—foreign-owned assembly plants.
plantation—a large estate or farm, usually worked by resident laborers.
terrain—physical features of a tract of land.

ment of large-scale, precious-metal mining. The most important mines were located in the mountains near the capital of Tegucigalpa. They were owned by the New York and Honduras Rosario Mining Company. Silver was the principal metal mined, accounting for about 55 percent of exports in the 1880s. Mining income improved the economy somewhat, but the mining industry never helped the country as a whole very much. The foreign mining companies employed a small workforce, paid little in taxes or export duties, and relied mostly on imported mining equipment.

In the first half of the 20th century, many Hondurans resented the vast banana plantations established by U.S. companies along the northern coast. In 1954, striking banana workers successfully fought for a labor code that, once drafted, became considered one of the most comprehensive in Central America. The code has generally resulted in a higher standard of living for workers and better operating conditions for businesses. Today, foreign fruit companies do not have the influence in Honduras they once did. However, labor laws are not always strictly applied, and some workplaces are substandard. Worker complaints have been especially loud in *maquiladoras*, or foreign-owned assembly plants, and in conjunction with lobster harvesting. In both cases, workers complain that their health is endangered by the conditions under which they are forced to work. Other complaints include low pay, abusive supervisors, and insufficient medical care.

An Improving Forecast

As Honduras entered the 1990s, signs that the country might be on the way to economic growth began to appear. First, a strong civilian government was able to act without interference from the military. Second, bananas were booming again, particularly as new European trade agreements created bigger markets. Small banana-producing businesses owned by workers lined up to sell their land to the commercial giants, and the last banana-producing lands held by the government were sold to private companies.

Like most of Central America, Honduras in the 1990s began to attract foreign *investors*, mostly Asian clothing assembly firms. (Look for clothes in discount stores with labels that say "Hecho en Honduras.") Burdened with a heavy national debt, aging industries, and poor roads and railroads, however, Honduras still faces economic disadvantages compared with its Central American and Caribbean neighbors, who compete with Honduras for overseas sales. Fortunately, major nations that Honduras owes money to are helping the government manage the debt and encourage more investment from abroad in new industries.

Today, Honduras's natural resources include rich pine forests and modest deposits of silver, lead, zinc, iron, gold, cadmium, antimony, and copper. But widespread slash-and-burn methods of creating farmland by destroying forests continue, and mineral exports are hampered by inadequate road and rail systems—most roads are unpaved. Industry, located chiefly in San Pedro Sula, is small and produces goods for local markets: processed food (mainly sugar and coffee), textiles, clothing, lumber, and wood products. On the other hand, new maquiladoras continue to open in Honduras, providing jobs for more than 150,000 workers.

Tourism also has great potential for generating income in Honduras. The clear, warm Caribbean waters are ideal for sport diving, and the coral-

Quick Facts: The Economy of Honduras

Gross Domestic Product (GDP): $39.23 billion
GDP per capita: $4,800 (2013)
Natural resources: timber, gold, silver, copper, lead, zinc, iron ore, antimony, coal, fish, hydropower.
Industry (28.2 percent of GDP): sugar, coffee, woven and knit apparel, wood products, cigars.
Agriculture (14 percent of GDP): bananas, coffee, citrus, corn, African palm; beef; timber; shrimp, tilapia, lobster.
Services (57.8 percent of GDP): tourism, other.

Annual Exports: $7.881 billion—apparel, coffee, shrimp, automobile wire harnesses, cigars, bananas, gold, palm oil, fruit, lobster, lumber.
Annual Imports: $11.34 billion—machinery and transport equipment, industrial raw materials, chemical products, fuels, foodstuffs.
Unemployment rate: 4.5 percent.
Economic growth rate: 2.8 percent (2013)
Currency exchange rate: 21.73 Honduran Lempras = U.S. $1 (2015)

* GDP or gross domestic product—the total value of goods and services produced in a year.
Sources: CIA World Factbook 2015; Bloomberg.com. All figures 2014 estimates, unless otherwise noted.

sand beaches and climate attract international vacationers. The famous Mayan ruins at Copán and the well-preserved colonial fort at Omoa also attract thousands of visitors each year. Unfortunately, the increase in gang violence in recent years has had a negative effect on the number of tourists that visit Honduras.

TEXT-DEPENDENT QUESTIONS

1. What are two major agricultural products from Honduras?
2. What are some complaints workers have about *maquiladoras*? About how many Hondurans are employed in these factories?

(Opposite) Hondurans shop at an outdoor vegetable market in the village of Copán Ruinas, which is not far from the ancient Mayan site. (Right) Amerindians perform a traditional dance welcoming visitors to Roatan Island, off the coast of Honduras. The island is a favorite stop for cruise lines.

4 The People of Honduras

AMONG THEMSELVES, Hondurans are known affectionately as *catrachos*. About 90 percent of the population are *mestizos*—Spanish-speaking persons of Indian-Spanish heritage. Most of the Indians are Lenca. They are found in the southwest, near the Guatemala border, close to the important Indian centers of the Mayan period. More than 100 years ago, immigrants from the Caribbean Islands settled in the lowlands and the Bay Islands. These are the Garifuna, or Black Caribs, who live in 44 coastal villages. Then, in the 1970s and 1980s, a new population—approximately 50,000 refugees—arrived in Honduras to escape the civil unrest in surrounding countries. Most are housed by the United Nations in camps near the borders, but numerous uncounted illegal refugees are scattered throughout the country.

Population Growth

Generally, the population of Honduras is concentrated in the interior highlands and in the Caribbean lowlands. Almost two-thirds of Hondurans live in rural areas. The largest urban centers are the capital, Tegucigalpa; San Pedro Sula, the center of industry and agriculture; La Ceiba, home of the former Standard Fruit Company; and Choluteca.

The population grew extremely fast during the mid-20th century posing a big problem in employment and housing. During the 1980s and 1990s, there was an especially rapid increase in urban population in and around Tegucigalpa, causing overcrowding in housing and air and water pollution. Although the rate of population growth in Honduras slowed by the late 1990s, it remained well above the world average. In the rest of the country, the mountainous, forested terrain and dirt roads isolate the rural poor.

Rural Life

Honduras is still one of the least urbanized countries of Central America. Rural residents are farmers, although about 60 percent of Honduran land

Words to Understand in this Chapter

Machete—a large, heavy broad-bladed knife used as a tool for cutting through vegetation.
Malnutrition—poor health and low weight caused by lack of food.
Squatter—a person who settles on property that he or she does not legally own.

remains covered with forest. Only 25 percent of the total land is available for agriculture or pastureland.

A vast majority of rural dwellers are small farmers who till their own plots or landless laborers who work for wages on estates or smaller farms. The move toward small farms increased rapidly after 1960 as the population grew. Because the peasants divided their land among all the sons, a farmer with six sons will divide an already-small farm six ways. Many peasants with plots of their own also seek part-time jobs to increase their incomes. For example, a man may work his father's land, rent additional land of his own, and do occasional day labor, too.

The steepness of the mountain slopes often makes agriculture impossible or at least extremely hard. It is estimated that almost 90 percent of the mountainous area of Honduras has slopes that barely support farm-

A modest home in rural Honduras. More than half of Honduras's population lives in poverty, and the country's per capita income is among the lowest in Latin America. Poverty rates are highest among rural and indigenous people.

ing or even grassland for animals. In addition, exhausted or poor soil and crop losses result in poverty for small farmers.

Part of the soil erosion and loss of soil fertility comes from the methods used in farming. To clear land, small farmers tend to use the slash-and-burn method. This consists of hacking down vegetation with *machetes* and then burning it. Using hoes, axes, digging sticks, and possibly wooden plows, they plant the ground without the use of fertilizer. A percentage of the harvest then ends up ruined because it is stored in unprotected facilities and eaten by rodents and pests.

Most of the rural people live in one- or two-room thatch-roofed huts (*bahareques*) built of adobe or sugarcane stalks and mud with dirt floors. The size of plantations and commercial cattle farms has grown in the last few decades, making it harder for peasants to find a plot of land suitable for a house. Many who once lived on the edges of larger estates were forced off the land. As a result, there is much "fence housing" in Honduras. A *squatter* and his family, squeezed off land by plantation crops, live in a tiny hut in the narrow space between a public road and the landowner's fence.

Living in poverty, most of the rural people exist on a plain but not very nutritious diet: corn tortillas, beans, cassava melons, plantains, rice, and coffee. Each rural household usually has pigs and chicken, but meat doesn't appear on the table very often, nor do green vegetables for that matter.

In fact, food production in Honduras has never been equal to the people's needs. Widespread *malnutrition* contributes to the population's fragile health. Although the food supply is just enough to subsist, it is not sufficient to promote good health. Hondurans often do not link infectious

Quick Facts: The People of Honduras

Population: 8,598,561

Ethnic groups: mestizo (mixed Amerindian and European) 90%, Amerindian 7%, black 2%, white 1%.

Age structure:
0–14 years: 34.8% percent
15–64 years: 61.3 percent
65 years and over: 3.9 percent

Population growth rate: 1.74 percent

Birth rate: 23.66 births/1,000 population

Death rate: 5.13 deaths/1,000 population

Infant mortality rate: 18.72 deaths/1,000 live births

Life expectancy at birth:
total population: 70.91 years
male: 69.24 years
female: 72.65 years

Total fertility rate: 2.86 children born per woman

Religions: Roman Catholic 97%, Protestant 3%.

Languages: Spanish (official), Amerindian dialects.

Literacy: 85.1% percent (2011 est.)

Source: CIA World Factbook 2015. All figures 2014 estimates, unless otherwise noted.

diseases, low birth weights, or mental retardation with poor diet and lack of sanitation. These problems have always existed in people's memories, so they tend to be accepted as normal.

Urban Life

Urban life in Honduras, as in many developing countries, points up the contrasts between the lifestyles of the well-off and the poor. Tegucigalpa and San Pedro Sula offer blocks of elegant apparel shops and jewelry stores. Tall office buildings provide headquarters for business and professional people who make up the rather small middle- and upper classes.

Did You Know?

- Honduras has a democratic constitutional government. Its current constitution became effective on January 20, 1982. It has been amended several times, most recently in 2013.
- The president is elected by popular vote to a four-year term. In 2014, Juan Orlando Hernandez was elected president of Honduras.
- There are 128 seats in Honduras's legislature, the *Congreso Nacional.* Members are elected by popular vote to serve four-year terms).
- The Supreme Court of Justice or *Corte Suprema de Justicia* consists of 15 judges elected for four-year terms by the National Congress.
- Major political parties in Honduras include the Liberal Party (PLH), National Party of Honduras (PNH), National Innovation and Unity Party (PINU), and the Christian Democratic Party (PDCH).
- The capital of Honduras is Tegucigalpa.
- The voting age is 18.
- The Honduran flag includes three horizontal bands (blue, white, and blue), with five blue, five-pointed stars centered on the white band

For most of Tegucigalpa's urban population, however, living conditions aren't much better than those of the rural poor. Unskilled job seekers coming to Tegucigalpa usually settle in the slums of the city center. When neighborhoods become too crowded, the slums, or *barrios*, creep outward toward the edges of the city. *Barrio* residents live in *cuarteríos*—unsanitary rows of windowless, dirt-floored rooms. The average household in the poor sections of cities often contains about seven persons in a single room, although sometimes a small kitchen stands in the rear covered by a tile overhang. Some *cuarterías* face the street, while others are arranged in double rows facing each other across a block-long alley, barely wide enough for a person to walk through. For those living in the rooms facing an alley, the narrow passageway between buildings serves both as a sewage and waste disposal area and as a courtyard for as many as 150 persons.

Relatives and friends tend to cluster together in the *barrios*, offering support to one another. But the pressures of poverty cause families to break apart, too. High unemployment forces parents to take migratory laboring jobs, moving around from place to place. Fathers desert their families, leaving the care and support of children entirely to mothers. Some children are abandoned to live on the streets. Beggar children haunt the airport in Tegucigalpa, for instance, rummaging through garbage and offering to carry tourists' luggage for tips.

The diet of the poor in the cities is only a little better than that of the rural poor, although open-air markets offer a greater variety of food. Many of the Hondurans who leave the country in search of work wind up in the United States, either as legal or illegal immigrants.

TEXT-DEPENDENT QUESTIONS

1. In what areas do almost two-third of Hondurans live?
2. What commonly used farming methods damage the soil in Honduras?
3. What is the largest city in Honduras?

(Opposite) Honduran goaltender Tursunbaev Akmal makes a save during an international match in Taiwan. Soccer is the favorite sport of many people of Honduras. (Right) Lime adds an accent to the food served at this traditional meal in Honduras.

5 Language, Religion, and Home Life

LANGUAGE, RELIGION, AND home life are the three central elements of Honduran culture. Spanish is the main language spoken throughout Honduras, although English is the language of choice in the Caribbean Islands. Most Hondurans are Roman Catholic, although there are many other churches, too, including Mormons, Jehovah's Witnesses, Seventh Day Adventists, Baptists, Pentecostals, Assemblies of God, and Evangelicals. Native Indian groups have their own religions, often blending elements of African and Indian ancestor-worship with Christian practices. Finally, the family is central to Honduran daily life and society, and strong emphasis is placed on family loyalty.

Signs of the Past

Any visitor to Honduras will notice that the art and architecture of the Mayan and Spanish colonial periods are strongly evident in Honduran culture. Of special interest to tourists, archeologists, and historians is the great Mayan city of Copán, which represents the height of the Mayan Classic period. Discovered in the early 16th century, Copán was partly excavated and restored in 1839. Spanish architecture in Honduras also reflects styles borrowed from 16th–18th century southern Europe.

Modern Honduran culture has not produced many examples of its own art, mainly because of the country's widespread poverty. Most artists re-create their Spanish heritage, and the Mayan past is seen chiefly in Indian crafts.

The Influence of the Catholic Church

The Roman Catholic Church has been a powerful institution in Honduras since colonial times. In the 1880s, the Honduran government tried to reduce the influence of the Roman Catholic Church by stripping it of some of its economic and political power. Nevertheless, in the 20th century the church actually enlarged its role in Honduran affairs, especially in regard to the rights of the poor.

In the 1950s, the Roman Catholic Church in Honduras launched a campaign to encourage church membership. During the 1960s and 1970s, local priests became outspoken critics of the military and the government's treatment of the poor. The tension reached a terrible pitch in 1975, when

In La Esparanza, traditional dancers take part in a celebration—a mock trial of Christopher Columbus, who is accused of destroying the native culture of Honduras.

landowners in Olancho murdered 10 peasants, two students, and two priests for organizing protests over land ownership and the wages paid to agricultural workers After this incident, the government took measures to stop the criticism. Expulsions and arrests of foreign priests took place, and some church-sponsored peasant centers were forced to close. The Roman Catholic Church retreated temporarily, but renewed its calls for reform in the 1980s.

Protestant churches have seen growth in membership in recent years. The largest numbers are found in Methodist, Church of God, Seventh Day Adventist, and Assemblies of God denominations. These churches sponsor social service programs in many communities, making them attractive to the poor.

Today, all church schools receive government funding, and religious instruction is part of the public school curriculum.

The Importance of the Family

The family is central to Honduran daily life and society. Family ties contribute to Hondurans' identity, and relatives help one another in business. Some family members add to the household income by learning crafts: woodcarving (notably wooden instruments), basketry, embroidery and textile arts, leather craft, and ceramics. These are sold on market days or in tourist areas.

Hondurans usually marry in religious ceremonies, but civil marriages performed by a judge are common, too. Many couples live together until they can afford a religious ceremony and a wedding celebration. Close, trusted friends are often brought into family circles by being designated *compadres* (godparents), an honor—and a responsibility—that is often given at marriages and baptisms.

In Honduran households, the meals are based around beans, rice,

The Los Dolores church in Tegucigalpa was built in 1735. Nearly all Hondurans observe the Roman Catholic religion, which was brought to Central America by the Spanish.

tortillas, fried bananas, meat, potatoes, cream, and cheese. Celebrations bring out specialty dishes, such as tamales and *yuca con chicharrón* (fried cassava and pork). There are also many *comidas típicas* (typical foods) special to various regions of the country, including *sopa de hombre* (man's soup) and seafood dishes in the south, *queso con chile* (cheese with chili peppers) in the west, and *cazabe* (mashed cassava) among Garifuna or Black Caribs in the Caribbean lowlands.

The gap between the wealthy (and even the middle class) and the poor is wide, especially in regards to food. The poor tend to rely on corn, often eaten as tortillas. Beans, cassava, plantains, and rice are common, but meat and green vegetables are not. Poor families in rural areas typically live on tiny parcels of land, and urban poor often live in cramped, unsanitary rows of dirt-floored rooms called *cuarteríos*.

A quiet street in Gracias, a small village not far from Celaque National Park.

Recreation and Sports

Hondurans listen to several radio stations featuring rock and popular music from the United States and Europe. Televisions are not common. Many television programs are imported and dubbed into Spanish, and motion pictures are usually Hollywood imports with Spanish subtitles. Family recreation often revolves around religious festivals honoring local saints. On February 3, for example, Catholics throughout the nation celebrate the patron saint of Honduras, the Virgin of Suyapa, named for the village near which her image was found.

Soccer is a passion of many Hondurans. There is hardly a village that does not sponsor a team or club at some level of competition. International matches attract the whole country's attention. In 1998, the Honduran national team advanced to the semifinals in the 1998 World Cup; it has qualified twice for the World Cup tournament since then, in 2010 and 2014. The national team, known as Los Catrachos, has won an annual tournament of Central American teams three times, in 1993, 1995, and 2011.

Honduras's better-quality sports and recreational facilities are used mainly by tourists. Scuba diving, swimming, and sport fishing are popular in the resort region around Cannon Island, on the northern coast.

Cultural institutions in Honduras include the National School of Music and the Republican History Museum, both in Tegucigalpa, and the Archaeological Museum of Comayagua. The Autonomous National University of Honduras, founded in 1847 in Tegucigalpa, enrolls more than 30,000 students. Small theaters produce plays in both Spanish and English.

TEXT-DEPENDENT QUESTIONS

1. What religious denomination has been a powerful force in Honduras since colonial times?
2. What are some specialty dishes eaten during celebrations?
3. What is the most popular sport in Honduras?

THERE ARE FESTIVITIES in just about every town to celebrate saints' days. The fair for the Virgen de Suyapa, patron saint of Honduras, is celebrated in Suyapa, 4 miles southeast of Tegucigalpa, during the first two weeks of February. Because of the number of Roman Catholics in the country, important celebrations revolve around such religious holidays as Christmas, the season of Lent, Holy Week, and Easter.

Other public holidays include New Year's Day (January 1), Panamerican Day (April 14), Labor Day (May 1), Independence Day (September 15), Francisco Morazan Day (October), Columbus Day (October 12), and Army Day (October 21).

Carnaval at La Ceiba is celebrated during the third week of May with parades, costumes, and street music. There are other popular fairs in Copán Ruinas (March 15–20), Tela (June 13), Trujillo (June 24), San Pedro Sula (last week in June), and Danlí (the last weekend in August).

The Feria Centroamericana de Tourismo y Artesanía, a Central American international artisans' and tourism fair, is held annually from December 6–16 in Tegucigalpa. Another cultural fair is held in Copán Ruins from December 15–21.

A school marching band performs during Independence Day festivities. Hondurans celebrate September 15 as the date Central America received its independence from Spain, although related festivities continue throughout the month.

Dulce de Leche

(Serves 3 to 4)
1 quart milk
1 cup sugar
1 tsp. vanilla
6 slices of white bread, torn into tiny pieces
2 egg yolks, beaten
Cinnamon to taste

Directions:

1. Cook the milk together with the sugar, vanilla, and cinnamon, and stir constantly.
2. When milk begins to thicken, add bread, and continue stirring.
3. When mixture gets thick, remove from heat, and beat thoroughly. While it is still warm, add the well-beaten egg yolks, and let the batch cool.
4. Refrigerate until ready to eat.

Guacamole

1 cup mashed avocado
1/4 cup mayonnaise
2 Tbs. lemon juice
1/4 cup finely chopped stuffed olives
1 Tbs. grated onion
1 tsp. salt
1/4 tsp. chili powder or cayenne
12 oz. bag of tortilla chips

Directions:

Combine mashed avocado, mayonnaise, lemon juice, olives, onion, and seasonings. Chill. Use as a dip for the chips.

Plantain Pancakes

(Serves 3 to 5)
3 very ripe plantains
3 Tbsp. flour
4 Tbsp. melted butter
2/3 cup cooked red kidney beans
2/3 cup shortening

Directions:

1. Boil and mash plantains. Add flour and butter, and mix thoroughly.
2. Fry the beans in 1 Tbsp. shortening for about 5 minutes.
3. Heat remaining shortening in another frying pan. Add plantain mixture, 1 Tbsp. at a time, and spread with a fork so that it will take the shape of a small pancake. Fry the pancakes for about 5 minutes. Place a teaspoon of the fried beans on each, and fold.
4. Fry the stuffed pancakes, covered, three minutes on each side or until brown.

Coconut Bread

(Serves 6 to 8)
1 lb. shredded coconut
3 cups all-purpose flour
1 Tbsp. baking powder
1/2 cup butter
1 cup sugar
2 eggs
2 tsp. salt

Directions:
1. Preheat oven to 350° F.
2. Mix dry ingredients in a large bowl.
3. Beat eggs and add to dry ingredients. Add melted butter.
4. Mix ingredients together. Add a little milk if the batch seems dry.
5. Pour into two lightly greased loaf pans or two lightly greased pie dishes.
6. Bake for about 40-45 minutes or until toothpick comes out clean from the center.

Rompopo (Honduran Eggnog)

(Serves 8 to 10)
1/2 gallon milk
8 egg yolks
1/4 cup sugar
3 large cinnamon sticks
2 cloves
Dash of pepper
1 cup white grape juice
Pinch of nutmeg

Directions:
1. In a big pot, boil milk together with sugar, cinnamon, nutmeg, and cloves.
2. In a bowl, separate yolks and whites, and beat the yolks.
3. Cook milk and yolks at medium heat, stirring constantly until the mixture loses its egg flavor. Let it cool, and add grape juice
4. Keep eggnog in a covered bowl, and refrigerate.
5. Do not add ice when serving eggnog.

Amerindian—a term for the indigenous peoples of North, Central, and South America before the arrival of Europeans in the late 15th century.

civil liberty—the right of people to do or say things that are not illegal without being stopped or interrupted by the government.

conquistador—any one of the Spanish leaders of the conquest of the Americas in the 1500s.

Communism—a political system in which all resources, industries, and property are considered to be held in common by all the people, with government as the central authority responsible for controlling all economic and social activity.

coup d'état—the violent overthrow of an existing government by a small group.

criollo—a resident of Spain's New World colonies who was born in North America to parents of Spanish ancestry. During the colonial period, criollos ranked above mestizos in the social order.

deforestation—the action or process of clearing forests.

economic system—the production, distribution, and consumption of goods and services within a country.

ecotourism—a form of tourism in which resorts attempt to minimize the impact of visitors on the local environment, contribute to conserving habitats, and employ local people.

embargo—a government restriction or restraint on commerce, especially an order that prohibits trade with a particular nation.

exploit—to take advantage of something; to use something unfairly.

foreign aid—financial assistance given by one country to another.

free trade—trade based on the unrestricted exchange of goods, with tariffs (taxes) only used to create revenue, not keep out foreign goods.

Mesoamerica—the region of southern North America that was inhabited before the arrival of the Spaniards.

mestizo—a person of mixed Amerindian and European (typically Spanish) descent.

plaza—the central open square at the center of colonial-era cities in Latin America.

plebiscite—a vote by which the people of an entire country express their opinion on a particular government or national policy.

population density—a measurement of the number of people living in a specific area, such a square mile or square kilometer.

pre-Columbian—referring to a time before the 1490s, when Christopher Columbus landed in the Americas.

regime—a period of rule by a particular government, especially one that is considered to be oppressive.

service industry—any business, organization, or profession that does work for a customer, but is not involved in manufacturing.

Maps

- Using a heavy piece of cardboard or poster board, first draw a large map of Honduras. Then, using a mixture of flour and paste, create three-dimensional mountain ranges. Refer to a topographical map that appears in an encyclopedia as a guide. Use watercolors to paint the mountain ranges when you're finished—be sure to label the ranges.

- Use a physical map of the United States or the world to locate states or countries with physical features similar to those of Honduras. Would the climate and lifestyle (food, clothing, leisure activities, livelihoods, etc.) of those areas be the same as that of Honduras? Why or why not?

- Locate and research the lifestyles of people living in various mountain regions around the world. Create a poster showing how people in mountainous regions share similar traits.

- Work in a small group to research the climate, resources, and cultures of cities in the United States that are at the same altitude as Tegucigalpa.

- Draw a large map of Honduras. Leave room in the margins to write one-paragraph descriptions of jungle or forest animals that live in Honduras. Draw or cut out pictures of these animals to go with your descriptions.

Flashcards

Using the glossary in this book, create flashcards. Put the term on one side and the definition on the other. Practice with the cards in pairs. Then, choose two teams of three. Select a referee to say the term out loud, and then call on someone to give the definition. The referee's decision is final. Award points for each correct answer. You can also read the definition, and ask for the correct term instead!

Short Reports

- Respond in writing to one or both of these questions: What is a rain forest? What does a rain forest have to do with me?
- Research the location and problems of rain forests in the United States. Compare the problems of deforestation in U.S. rain forests with the problems of deforestation in Honduras.
- Write a one-page report on Hurricane Mitch, which hit Honduras in 1998.
- Write a short report on the contras: Who were they? Why did the United States support them?
- Write a short report on William Walker: Who was he? Why was he trying to take over Central America?

Projects

- Using a picture of a Mayan temple, build a small-scale model or show what Copán looks like from the air.
- Using the same picture, re-create a Mayan glyph using model clay. Make it about the size of a textbook lying flat.

1000 BCE	The Maya settle at Copán in western Honduras.
600–900 CE	Mayan culture is at its strongest.
1502	Columbus sets foot on the American mainland for the first time at Trujillo in northern Honduras; he names the country after the deep water off the Caribbean coast.
1520	Spanish conquistadors and a few settlers begin arriving.
1538	Chief of the Lenca tribe, Lempira, who is leading 30,000 Indians against the Spanish, is murdered during peace talks.
1570	Adventurers discover gold and silver near Tegucigalpa.
1643	Dutch pirates loot and burn Trujillo.
1821	Spain grants independence to Honduras.
1860	American adventurer, William Walker, who attempts to take over Central America, is defeated in Trujillo by an army of Hondurans, Nicaraguans, and Costa Ricans.
1920–1923	Seventeen uprisings or attempted government overthrows in Honduras give rise to the term "banana republic."
1932–1954	Honduras is ruled by two dictators: Tiburcio Carías Andino and Juan Manuel Gálvez.
1956	The military ousts the president of Honduras. It will continue to manage Honduran politics for decades.
1969	Six-day Soccer War with El Salvador over alleged mistreatment of El Salvadoran immigrants in Honduras.

1980	Honduran refugee camps serve as military training grounds for U.S.-aided troops fighting Communist-supported governments in surrounding countries; the Contras become a major political issue in the United States.
1980–1990	To safeguard native plants and animals, the Honduras government establishes national parks, protected forests, and biological reserves.
1998	Hurricane Mitch slams into Honduras, killing 5,000 people and causing $3 billion in damage.
2002	Newly elected president Ricardo Maduro takes office in January.
2003	Although much of Hurricane Mitch's destruction has been repaired, Honduras remains the poorest country in Central America.
2006	Manuel Zelaya begins a four-year term as president of Honduras.
2009	Zelaya is removed by the military and forced into exile. The coup is condemned by the international community.
2010	Porfirio "Pepe" Lobo Sosa of the National Party is sworn in as president. The United States and other countries resume aid to Honduras, deeming a return to democracy.
2014	In January, Juan Orlando Hernandez is sworn in as president. In May, Honduras turns suspected drug lord Carlos Arnoldo Lobo over to the United States.
2015	The US increases aid to Honduras to help combat gang violence and drug smuggling.

Further Reading/Internet Resources

Benchwick, Greg. *Honduras and the Bay Islands.* Oakland, Calif.: Lonely Planet, 2010.

Booth, John A., et al. *Understanding Central America: Global Forces, Rebellion, and Change*, 5th ed. Boulder, Colo.: Westview Press, 2009.

Heuman, Gad. *The Caribbean: A Brief History.* New York: Bloomsbury, 2014.

McGaffey, Zeta, and Michael Spilling. *Honduras.* New York: Marshall Cavendish, 2010.

Williamson, Edwin. *The Penguin History of Latin America.* New York: Penguin Group, 2010.

Culture and Festivals

http://www.everyculture.com/Ge-It/Honduras.html
http://www.lonelyplanet.com/honduras

Economic and Political Information

http://www.state.gov/p/wha/ci/ho
https://www.cia.gov/library/publications/the-world-factbook/geos/ho.html
http://lanic.utexas.edu/

History and Geography

http://memory.loc.gov/frd/cs/hntoc.html#hn0004
http://www.history.com/topics/maya

Travel information

http://www.worldtravelguide.net/honduras
http://www.honduras.com/

American Field Service (AFS) Honduras
Colonia El Castaño
Avenida Los Castaños
Casa 2941
Apartado Postal 1300
Tegucigalpa, Honduras
Phone: (504) 232-5202
Fax: (504) 2239-5130
Website: www.afs.hn
Email: info-honduras@afs.org

Caribbean/Latin American Action
1625 K Street NW, Suite 200
Washington, DC 20006
Phone: (202) 464-2031
Website: www.c-caa.org

Embassy of Honduras
3007 Tilden Street, N.W.
Washington, D.C. 20008
Phone: (202) 966-7702
Fax: (202) 966-9751
Website:www.hondurasemb.org
Email: embassy@hondurasemb.org

U.S. Department of Commerce
International Trade Administration
Office of Latin America and the Caribbean
1401 Constitution Ave., NW
Washington, D.C. 20230
Phone: (202) 482-2000
Fax: (202) 482-5168
Website: www.commerce.gov
Email: publicaffairs@doc.gov

U.S. Agency for International Development
Ronald Reagan Building
Washington, D.C. 20523-0001
Phone: (202) 712-0000
Website: www.usaid.gov
Email: pinquiries@usaid.gov

Embassy of Guatemala
2220 R Street NW
Washington, DC 20008
Phone: (202) 232-2226

Contributors

Senior Consulting Editor **James D. Henderson** is professor of international studies at Coastal Carolina University. He is the author of *Conservative Thought in Twentieth Century Latin America: The Ideals of Laureano Gómez* (1988; Spanish edition *Las ideas de Laureano Gómez* published in 1985); *When Colombia Bled: A History of the Violence in Tolima* (1985; Spanish edition *Cuando Colombia se desangró, una historia de la Violencia en metrópoli y provincia*, 1984); and co-author of *A Reference Guide to Latin American History* (2000) and *Ten Notable Women of Latin America* (1978).

    Mr. Henderson earned a bachelors degree in history from Centenary College of Louisiana, and a masters degree in history from the University of Arizona. He then spent three years in the Peace Corps, serving in Colombia, before earning his doctorate in Latin American history in 1972 at Texas Christian University.

Charles J. Shields, the author of all eight books in the DISCOVERING CENTRAL AMERICA series, lives in Homewood, a suburb of Chicago, with his wife Guadalupe, an elementary-school principal. He has a degree in history from the University of Illinois in Urbana-Champaign, and was chairman of the English department and the guidance department at Homewood-Flossmoor High School in Flossmoor, Illinois.